100 THINGS TO DO IN PLANO BEFORE YOU DIE

Reedy Press
PO Box 5131
St. Louis, MO 63139, USA
reedypress.com

Library of Congress Control Number: 2025949911
ISBN: 9781681066318

Design by Jill Halpin

Cover photo courtesy of Visit Plano

Unless otherwise noted, all photos are courtesy of the author or are believed to be in the public domain.

Printed in the United States of America
26 27 28 29 30   5 4 3 2 1

100 THINGS TO DO IN PLANO BEFORE YOU DIE

ABBIE ALTER

REEDY PRESS

Oak Point Recreation Center and Pool
Credit Cassie Clair

DEDICATION

To my kids and my husband's job: Without you, I'd never have landed in Plano, Texas, or learned how to pronounce y'all properly.

Legacy West Fountain
Credit Visit Plano

CONTENTS

Culture and History

Shopping and Fashion

ACKNOWLEDGMENTS

To my husband, Daniel, for bringing us here in the first place and allowing me to flourish as an entrepreneur and now as a writer. And to my kids, Jesse and Lucy, who've grown up here without forgetting their roots, and were always willing to let me take endless photos, at least before they became teenagers.

A huge thank-you to the team of moms who work with me, the Plano Moms online community, and the readers of planomoms.com. Your support, feedback, and energy have shaped this book and my journey through Plano. Together, we've built something truly special.

To the many community leaders whom I now count as friends—you inspired my involvement in local nonprofits and continue to show what real service and passion look like. From all walks of life, you make Plano better for everyone. Special shout-out to the BABBS—you know who you are.

Thank you to the local organizations who generously shared photography for this book—it's an honor to include your work. And to Jennifer Shertzer, who is one of many unsung heroines of Plano life. Thank you.

Here's to all the local small business owners whose businesses are listed in the pages of this book, and to the readers of this book, who I hope will get to Plano as soon as they can.

Shops at Legacy *Texas Loves Yall* Mural
Credit Shops at Legacy

PREFACE

I'm the ultimate transplant, moving to Plano, Texas, with my husband's job, all the way from London, England. I had two young kids, arrived with a lot of luggage and a million questions, and didn't know a soul. Twelve years later, I've raised my kids here, made lifelong friends, and built a deep love for the place I never expected to call home.

Over that time, I've explored every inch of this city—72 square miles filled with surprises. Who knew you could shop for Chanel at Legacy West and pick out your first pair of cowboy boots at Cavender's, all in one afternoon? You can float a lazy river, zip-line through the treetops, play pickleball, or hear a live symphony. There's live music, stand-up comedy, schnitzels, fresh seafood—even London-worthy Indian food if you know where to look.

Native Texans now share neighborhoods with newcomers from all over the US and the world. What was once a Dallas suburb is now a fully fledged city where you can live, work, and play without driving more than 20 minutes in any direction. And there's something for everyone, from babies in strollers to active seniors.

This book is a love letter to the Plano I've come to know. Whether you're new in town or a lifelong resident, I hope these 100 things spark your curiosity and inspire you to explore all the layers of this unique, welcoming place I now call home.

Lexus Box Garden Legacy Hall

FOOD AND DRINK

1

SAVOR THE FLAVORS
AT LEGACY HALL

If you love variety and can never settle on just one cuisine, Legacy Hall is your dream dining destination. This three-story hot spot in Plano's Legacy West district offers more than 20 artisanal food stalls, bars, and dessert counters, all under one roof.

You'll find everything from Texas-style dry-rub brisket to plant-based burgers, Neapolitan pizzas, poke bowls, crepes, and craft tacos. Whether you're gluten free, vegan, or just adventurous, there's something on the menu for everyone. Don't skip dessert. You'll find whimsical treats like shaved ice and cotton candy that kids (and grown-ups) love.

Meals are made to order and typically ready within 15 to 20 minutes, making this a fast-casual experience without sacrificing quality. Grab a seat indoors in the air-conditioning or head outside to the Lexus Box Garden, the venue's open-air patio with communal seating, twinkle lights, and a lively stage. Legacy Hall hosts live music, themed nights, and family-friendly events nearly every evening and weekend, making it more of an experience.

7800 Windrose Ave., 972-846-4255
legacyfoodhall.com

2

ENJOY OLD-WORLD CHARM

AT JÖRG'S CAFÉ VIENNA

Housed in a historic building in Downtown Plano, Jörg's Café Vienna has been a beloved neighborhood staple for over two decades. This cozy, family-owned restaurant brings a taste of Austria to Texas, serving up traditional dishes from recipes passed down through generations.

Inside, you'll find charming old-world decor and personal touches that reflect the owners' Austrian roots—think vintage beer steins, travel photos, and family memorabilia. The food is just as authentic. Wiener schnitzels, wursts, goulash, red cabbage, spaetzle, and apple strudel are menu standouts, with hearty flavors that feel like a warm hug on a plate. Don't miss the house-made cream schnitzel or a glass of Austrian rosé that's nearly impossible to find elsewhere in North Texas.

It's a rare and delightful experience and a European escape just steps from Haggard Park.

1037 E 15th St., 972-509-5966
jorgscafevienna.com

3

SAVOR URBAN CRUST

Let me introduce you to what I consider the crown jewel of Plano's Italian scene. Urban Crust isn't just another pizza place—it's where wood-fired perfection meets downtown energy. The space itself, with its exposed brick and rooftop dining area, adds something special to every visit.

Their pizzas emerge from that 900-degree wood-burning oven with perfectly blistered crusts that strike that magical balance between chewy and crispy. While the classic Margherita never disappoints, I'd strongly recommend trying their more creative options—the truffle oil and prosciutto combinations here aren't just trendy add-ons, they're thoughtfully crafted flavor profiles. They also have a great drinks menu—so don't miss out on that.

1006 E 15th St., 972-509-1400
urbancrust.com

TIP

Head up to their rooftop bar around sunset. There's something magical about enjoying a craft cocktail and watching the sky change colors over Downtown Plano while waiting for your pizza to arrive. It's equally perfect for date night or a casual weekend brunch with friends.

DINE AT PLANO'S COZIEST ITALIAN SPOTS

Covino's Pasta & Pizza

A family-run favorite in Plano for over 20 years, known for its famous garlic knots and hearty, homestyle Italian dishes.

3265 Independence Pkwy., 972-519-0345
covinos.com

Little Rome Ristorante & Pizzeria

This cozy neighborhood spot offers classic Italian comfort food along with a replica leaning tower of Pisa in a warm, casual setting.

2707 W 15th St., Ste. B, 972-449-7071
thelittlerome.com

Mama's Pizza

Eat your pizza buffet-style, load up from the salad bar, and for something different, try any of the simple but tasty pastas.

2130 W Parker Rd., 972-596-3303
mamaspizzaplano.com

Taverna Rossa

This hot spot combines craft pizza with live music and local beer in a vibrant atmosphere, complete with a fun patio overlooking fountains.

4005 Preston Rd., Ste. 512, 972-403-3321
tavernarossa.com

Enzo's Italian Deli

This deli-style experience has stacked sandwiches, imported Italian goods, and a loyal local following. Couple it with the perfect wine pairing, thanks to its next-door neighbor, Corner Wines.

4017 Preston Rd., Ste. 535, 972-403-9463

4

STEP BACK IN TIME
AT MAMA'S DAUGHTERS' DINER

Mama's Daughters' Diner serves up classic comfort food with a side of nostalgia. Walking through the doors feels like entering a retro 1950s diner straight out of *Grease*, complete with friendly servers, cozy booths, and bottomless mugs of strong coffee that invite you to linger. It's family-owned and -operated, and that warmth shows in every detail.

Breakfast is the real star here, especially if you're craving a true Texas-sized plate. Think chicken-fried steak, grits, fluffy pancakes, homemade biscuits, cornbread, or the beloved "Mama's rolls." And save room for pie. If you're counting calories, this may not be your place, but if you love taking dessert home for later, you'll be very happy.

This local favorite has been featured on *Good Morning Texas* and in *Southern Living*, and for good reason.

6509 W Park Blvd., #400, 972-473-8877
mamasdaughtersdiner.com

TIP

Skip the Sunday after-church rush if you want a booth and a relaxed meal.

5

RAISE A STEIN
AT BAVARIAN GRILL

Perfect for anyone who loves hearty comfort food and a festive dose of gemütlichkeit, Bavarian Grill delivers a truly authentic German dining experience in a restaurant as big as Texas. From crispy schnitzels and juicy bratwursts to warm pretzels and rotating seasonal dishes, every bite feels like a passport stamp to southern Germany.

Bring a group and soak in the charm. There's a model train circling above your head, costumed servers welcoming you with cheer, and live accordion music from Jim, who might serenade you with "Edelweiss" or the "Bier Barrel Polka." The beer selection is just as memorable, featuring imported German brews on tap that pair perfectly with the lively atmosphere.

This Plano institution is more than just a restaurant. It's a cultural experience that keeps locals coming back for a little slice of Europe in North Texas.

3425 Premier Dr., 972-881-0705
bavariangrill.com

TIP

Don't come here if you're in a rush. This is a whole experience, and the speed of the service reflects that!

6

CATCH THE FRESHEST FLAVORS

AT URBAN SEAFOOD COMPANY

When you have to have seafood done right, Urban Seafood Company brings the coast to Downtown Plano with style. This chef-driven restaurant serves up everything from wood-grilled fish and shellfish to buttery lobster rolls and freshly shucked oysters that are worth the trip alone.

Order a chilled seafood tower to share, or explore the day's freshest offerings straight from the market board, often featuring off-menu surprises you won't want to miss. For home chefs, the in-house fish market lets you take the experience home with high-quality, sustainable catches prepped and ready to cook. The oyster bar is also a huge favorite with locals.

It's a neighborhood favorite that makes seafood feel both elevated and approachable, perfect for date nights, celebrations, or just treating yourself midweek.

1104 E 14th St., 214-251-8771
urbanseafoodcompany.com

TIP

This oyster bar is our favorite in the area! Combine some featured oysters with a lobster roll for a perfect seafood meal. Check the chalkboard for the catch of the day—seasonal fish and specials that often sell out before dinner ends.

7

START YOUR MORNING RIGHT
AT EDDIE'S DINER

Tucked away in a no-frills shopping center, Eddie's Diner is one of those under-the-radar spots locals swear by. Step inside and you'll be greeted with warm smiles, lightning-fast service, and a cozy, come-as-you-are vibe that makes everyone feel like a regular, even on your first visit.

The menu is classic diner fare with a Texas twist. The Tex-Mex omelet is packed with bold flavor, while the hearty chicken-fried steak breakfast comes piled high with eggs, pancakes, and fruit—you'll be full till dinner. If you're craving something lighter, the avocado toast is a personal favorite, perfectly seasoned and satisfying. And for serious breakfast fans, the Baconator omelet is a must-try with grits (just ask my friend who orders it every time).

4709 W Parker Rd., Ste. 425, 469-931-2353
eddiesdiner.co

TIP

Get there early on weekends—it fills up fast, but the service is so efficient, the wait never feels long.

SIP, PLAY, AND GIVE BACK
AT LOCAL GOOD COFFEE CO.

Plano's newest coffee spot is so much more than a café—it's a community hub with a mission. Local Good Coffee Co. brews up excellent coffee (from Lemma Coffee Co), ice cream from Local Creamery Plano, and tasty bites from local favorites like Hugs Cafe and the Empanada Cookhouse. But what really sets this place apart is its commitment to making Plano better. Every purchase helps support local families through the Local Good Pantry and Center, so your morning coffee is doing real good in the neighborhood.

Bring the kids for indoor play or relax on the spacious, covered patio while friends hit the pickleball, volleyball, or basketball courts—free and first come, first served. The atmosphere is open, welcoming, and full of positive energy, with workspaces, event rentals, and regular community events like open mic nights, paint parties, or Mommy and Me music mornings.

201 Legacy Dr., 469-925-0599
localgoodcoffee.com

BITE INTO BURGER BLISS
AT KENNY'S BURGER JOINT

Craving the best burger in Plano? Locals will point you straight to Kenny's Burger Joint. From the moment you cross the parking lot, the irresistible aroma of sizzling beef draws you in like a magnet. Inside, it's all about bold flavors, comfort food done right, and options that cater to everyone at the table.

The menu stars juicy, handcrafted burgers that are grilled to perfection and packed with personality. Try yours with a side of crispy fried pickles or the wildly popular bacon jalapeño poppers. Vegetarian? No problem—Kenny's happily swaps the patty for a savory grilled portobello mushroom that's anything but an afterthought. And if you're low carb or keto, you can wrap any burger or sandwich in crisp lettuce without sacrificing flavor.

They also have monthly specials to give you some variety with your burger choice to satisfy your taste buds.

5809 Preston Rd., Ste. 588, 972-378-0999
kennysburgerjoint.com

TIP

Don't skip the bar menu. This isn't just a burger joint. The martini selection is worth a visit on its own.

10

SIP AND SHARE
AT SIXTY VINES

Sixty Vines isn't just a restaurant—it's a whole vibe. With airy, high-ceilinged spaces, a sun-drenched greenhouse room, and a menu built for sharing, it's the perfect place to gather your crew for a casually sophisticated night out. Whether you're celebrating, catching up, or just wine curious, this is the kind of spot that feels like a mini escape, especially in spring or summer.

Start your meal with the golden truffle fries (you won't want to share, but you should), and no matter what you order, save room for the citrus olive oil cake. Wine lovers can sample from an impressive selection on tap, while mocktail fans are treated just as thoughtfully with custom-crafted creations.

3701 Dallas Pkwy., 469-620-8463
sixtyvines.com

TIP

Book early if you want to seat a group or prefer a table in the greenhouse. This is a popular choice, especially for groups of girlfriends and wine lovers.

11

TREAT YOURSELF
AT SWEET HUT BAKERY

Sweet Hut Bakery brings a taste of Atlanta's favorite Asian dessert spot right into the heart of Plano's bustling Asia Town. Just steps from a massive Asian grocery store, it's a perfect place to grab something sweet, sip a boba tea, and soak in the modern, lounge-worthy vibe. Whether you're working remotely or catching up with friends, this spot was built for lingering.

The glass display cases are filled with beautifully crafted pastries: fluffy buns, creamy custards, and savory snacks that rotate daily. The drink menu is just as tempting, offering a choice of teas and creative boba blends to satisfy any craving. With booth-style workstations, fast Wi-Fi, and a cozy patio for breezy afternoons, it's an easy place to make your own.

2001 Coit Rd., Ste. 301, 972-905-5533
sweethutbakery.com

TIP

Try the milk tea slush with tapioca and grab a savory pork floss bun. You won't regret it.

12

SAVOR TRADITIONAL TEX-MEX

AT EL PUEBLITO MEXICAN COCINA

El Pueblito isn't just another Tex-Mex joint. If you're looking for true Mexican authenticity, inspired by family recipes from Jalisco, Mexico, this is your place. Hiding in a corner of the Cross Creek shopping center at Alma and 15th, this cozy spot serves up homestyle Mexican dishes with a warm welcome and plenty of flavor. From sizzling fajitas and tender carnitas to enchiladas dripping with homemade sauce, the food here is fresh, with big portions and full of soul.

It's the kind of place where regulars are greeted by name and newcomers quickly feel like part of the *familia*. Weekends are especially lively with colorful cocktails (we love our margs!) and tables packed with families sharing plates and stories. And if you're lucky enough to visit on a molcajete night, don't miss the bubbling lava stone bowls filled with grilled meats and melted cheese—it's a feast and a show all in one.

901 Spring Creek Pkwy., #125, 972-527-6289
elpueblitomexicancocina.com

TIP

Be sure to try as many of their margaritas as you can, and get a designated driver too!

13

RAISE A GLASS
AT CORNER WINES

Corner Wines is the kind of place that makes wine feel friendly, not fussy. Tucked into a quiet Plano shopping center, it's a beloved neighborhood hangout where the staff knows your name and your taste in reds or whites. Whether you're popping in for a gift bottle or staying for a wine tasting or charcuterie class, the vibe is always warm and welcoming.

Ensure you stay on the mailing list and keep tabs on the new choices the store picks and sources globally, and also make sure to check out the menu. Just get into conversation with the owner and his team, and they'll be sure to suggest just the right bottle, for yourself or a gift for someone else.

Bonus: The cozy event space is ideal for small gatherings, girls' nights, or a casual date with flavor and flair. We have taken charcuterie classes here, which are perfect to pair with the wide choice of wines available.

4017 Preston Rd., Ste. 535, 972-403-9463
cornerwines.com

14

CHILL OUT
AT KATY TRAIL ICE HOUSE OUTPOST

Looking for laid-back vibes and serious patio goals? Katy Trail Ice House Outpost in Plano delivers. This offshoot of the Dallas favorite brings the same Texas-sized energy with an expanded, shaded patio that's made for lingering. With a mix of picnic tables, lounge seating, and plenty of room to spread out, it's one of the best spots in town to kick back with friends.

Order a round of spicy margaritas or a bucket of cold beer, and don't skip the loaded fries—they're the kind of messy deliciousness that pairs perfectly with casual conversation and good company. Despite being near a busy street and parking lot, the space is cleverly designed to feel like its own little hideaway, complete with misting fans that keep things cool even in the Texas heat.

4700 W Park Blvd., 972-599-9000
katyoutpost.com

TIP

It's first come, first served. Go early to claim the best patio spot.

15

KICK BACK
AT THE FILLMORE PUB

For an authentic pub vibe in the heart of Downtown Plano, the Fillmore Pub checks all the boxes. It's cozy, friendly, and just the right amount of lively, offering a well-stocked bar with a solid lineup of beers, ciders, and comforting pub fare. Think sliders stacked high, golden steak fries, and a menu that pairs perfectly with your pint.

What sets it apart is its unbeatable location. Just steps from McCall Plaza, it's the ideal pre- or postshow hangout. Grab a seat on the shaded, tree-lined patio and enjoy the sounds of live music drifting your way. Inside, challenge a friend to a game of darts and soak in the relaxed, neighborhood feel that keeps locals coming back.

It's also a great place to eat or grab a drink if you arrive early to park for any of the famous Downtown Plano festivals and events.

1004 E 15th St., 972-423-2400
thefillmorepub.com

16

SIP AND SAVOR ON THE PATIO
AT MI COCINA

At the Lakeside Market location of Mi Cocina, it's not just about the food—it's the whole experience. The patio here is a hidden gem, with tables overlooking peaceful fountains and just enough breeze to make your margarita taste even better. It's one of those spots where you could linger for hours, and many do.

Mi Cocina has earned its reputation as a go-to for upscale Tex-Mex in Plano. The chicken and steak fajitas come out sizzling and tender, and the sunset enchiladas are a local favorite—rich, flavorful, and satisfying. But let's be honest, no visit is complete without a margarita (or two). From classic to mango to the legendary "Mambo Taxi," there's a flavor for every mood.

4001 Preston Rd., 469-467-8655
micocina.com

TIP

Arrive early on weekends. The patio fills up fast for good reason.

17

SAVOR PARISIAN FLAVORS
AT TOULOUSE CAFE AND BAR

Transport yourself to the heart of Paris, with no passport required, at Toulouse Cafe and Bar in Legacy West. With its charming bistro decor, sidewalk seating, and soft glow from globe lights, this spot feels effortlessly chic yet completely approachable. The menu brings classic French dishes to life, from delicate crepes and buttery escargot to perfectly crisp duck confit and steak frites.

It's a favorite for brunch with friends, date nights, or just a cozy afternoon with a cappuccino and a croissant. Don't miss the signature French onion soup or the decadent profiteroles for dessert. Enjoy sipping rosé on the patio or enjoying live jazz during weekend brunch.

7301 Windrose Ave., Ste. C150, 972-943-6216
toulousecafeandbar.com

TIP

Try to snag a table on the patio during golden hour for the perfect Parisian vibe. It also makes a great spot for people watching as they meander along the Legacy West walkways.

Love & War in Texas
Credit Jennifer Shertzer

MUSIC AND ENTERTAINMENT

CATCH LIVE MUSIC
AT TAVERNA ROSSA

Taverna Rossa is more than just a great spot for craft pizza and cold beer. It's also a lively music venue that keeps the good vibes going every weekend. Every Friday and Saturday night from 7:30 to 10:30 p.m., the stage lights up with local and regional bands playing everything from country and classic rock to acoustic sets and bluesy jams. The cozy, rustic atmosphere, paired with good food and great music, makes this West Plano hangout a go-to spot for a casual night out.

Grab a table on the patio when the weather's nice, order one of the signature pizzas (try the Spicy Pig for something entirely different from any other pizza you've ever had), and settle in for an evening of toe-tapping tunes. It's family-friendly early in the evening, then shifts into more of a grown-up groove later on.

4005 Preston Rd., Ste. 512, 972-403-3321
tavernarossa.com/live-music

19

CATCH A SHOW
AT McCALL PLAZA

Small but mighty, McCall Plaza is one of Plano's most charming outdoor music venues. Tucked into the heart of historic Downtown Plano, this open-air stage regularly hosts live music, karaoke nights, and special events that bring the community together under the stars. With its BYOB policy and intimate atmosphere, it's the perfect place to kick back with your favorite drink and enjoy a night of entertainment.

The plaza's lineup often includes local bands, themed performances, and family-friendly gatherings, all surrounded by brick-lined streets and some of Plano's best restaurants and bars. Bring a lawn chair, arrive early to grab a good spot, and make a night of it in one of the city's most walkable and vibrant neighborhoods.

998 E 15th St., 972-941-5600
plano.gov/1080/McCall-Plaza

TIP

Along with your lawn chair, bring a cooler with ice for drinks and grab a take-out pizza from Urban Crust to enjoy during the show!

20

ROCK OUT
AT THE LEXUS BOX GARDEN AT LEGACY HALL

The Lexus Box Garden at Legacy Hall is Plano's ultimate backyard concert venue. This open-air space is packed with energy—think cover bands that get the whole crowd singing, a lively mosh pit, rows of picnic tables, and VIP lounges on upper levels that you can reserve for a premium experience. With a full lineup of concerts, themed parties, and movie nights, there's always something happening under the string lights.

Grab your dinner and drinks from any of the food stalls or bars inside Legacy Hall, then head outside for the show. Many events are ticketed, especially on weekends, and seating fills up quickly, so arrive early to secure a good spot. It also hosts occasional movie nights, including family-friendly favorites projected on the big stage screen.

7800 Windrose Ave., 972-846-4255
legacyfoodhall.com/lexus-box-garden

TIP

Shows typically wrap up by 10 p.m. to keep the peace with nearby residents, but that just means an early start to your evening of fun.

SING YOUR HEART OUT AT KARAOKE SPOTS IN PLANO

SPACE Karaoke Bar & Café

Perfect for private group nights, SPACE Karaoke offers sleek rooms, strong soundproofing, and an enormous song selection that spans languages and genres. It's a go-to for birthdays, celebrations, or just a fun night out with friends.

121 W Spring Creek Pkwy., Ste. 331, 214-430-0480
longhengdallasktv.com

II Brothers Grill & Bar

This laid-back neighborhood bar brings out the local talent on karaoke nights, along with great food, drink specials, and a fun crowd. It's a casual, no-pressure place to sing your favorite tunes.

8308 Preston Rd., 972-712-8308
iibrothers.com

Lantern St. Grill & Tap House

Known for its nightly karaoke (except Mondays and Tuesdays), Lantern St. adds pool tables and pub eats to the mix, making it a great all-around hangout. Expect a lively scene and lots of regulars.

6205 Coit Rd., Ste. 148, 469-814-0249
lanternst.com

Austin Avenue Grill & Sports Bar

Karaoke lights up this sports bar on Friday nights from 9 p.m. to 1 a.m., drawing a fun-loving adult crowd. There are also billiards, plenty of screens, and a full menu to round out your visit.

935 W Parker Rd., 972-422-8003
austinavenue.com

21

UNWIND WITH LIVE MUSIC
AT PLANO SPORTS TAVERN

Plano Sports Tavern is a true neighborhood hangout. It's unpretentious, lively, and packed with regulars who know how to have a good time. On weekend nights, the space transforms into a local music hub with live bands playing everything from classic rock and country to pop covers and upbeat party tunes. There's no cover charge, making it one of the most accessible spots in town for enjoying live entertainment without breaking the bank.

In addition to the music, you'll find pool tables, TVs tuned to the big game, and a full bar with rotating drink specials. The vibe is relaxed and welcoming, with a dance floor that fills up fast when the bands start to play. It's a great pick for a casual night out with friends, especially if you like your music loud and your evenings low-key.

3000 Custer Rd., 972-599-7598
planosportstavern.com

22

TWO-STEP INTO TEXAS CULTURE
AT LOVE & WAR IN TEXAS

If you're looking for a true taste of Texas, Love & War in Texas delivers with a side of live country music and line dancing. This Plano staple is more than just a restaurant; it's a celebration of Lone Star culture. With a large outdoor stage and regular performances from Texas-based artists, it's a favorite spot for catching rising country stars and well-loved local acts in an authentic, laid-back setting.

On the weekends, the patio fills with music lovers ready to dance under the stars, and you'll often see line dancing breaking out right in front of the stage. Inside, the menu pays homage to regional flavors from across Texas, so you can dig into a chicken-fried steak or smoked brisket while soaking in the music. Whether you're a seasoned two-stepper or just here for the show, this is classic Texas fun.

601 E Plano Pkwy., Ste. 100, 469-443-0015
loveandwarintexas.com

23

DANCE AND SING ALONG
AT SAMBUCA 360

Located in the Shops at Legacy, Sambuca 360 brings high-energy nightlife to Plano with a polished yet playful vibe. This is the spot for adults looking to let loose, whether you're singing your heart out during Tuesday night live-band karaoke or dancing to themed DJ sets and live acts on Friday and Saturday nights. The music is loud, the lights are low, and the party always feels just right.

The space features a small dance floor, cozy booths, and an upscale bar, making it a great choice for date nights, birthdays, or just a fun evening with friends. While drinks can be on the pricier side, the food (especially the shared plates and flatbreads) consistently gets high marks from regulars. It's probably the closest to a nightclub environment that you'll find in Plano.

7200 Bishop Rd., Ste. 270, 469-467-3393
sambucalive360.com

TIP

Be sure to follow Sambuca 360 on social media and its website for the fun events it plans year-round.

EXPERIENCE LIVE MUSIC
WITH THE PLANO SYMPHONY ORCHESTRA

The Plano Symphony Orchestra brings world-class music to the heart of North Texas, blending classical excellence with a warm, community-oriented atmosphere. Whether you're a long-time subscriber or attending for the first time, you'll find the experience both accessible and inspiring. The orchestra performs at several venues throughout the region, including the beautiful Robinson Fine Arts Center in Plano and the renowned Meyerson Symphony Center in Dallas.

In addition to its regular concert season, the PSO offers a Family Series that introduces younger audiences to the magic of live music through interactive, engaging performances designed with kids in mind. It also hosts educational programs and community outreach events, making music more accessible to audiences of all ages. With exceptional musicianship and a strong emphasis on audience connection, the PSO continues to be one of the area's most treasured cultural gems.

972-473-7262
planosymphony.org

25

SOAK UP THE SOUNDS

WITH OUTDOOR CONCERTS AT HAGGARD PARK

There's nothing quite like a warm summer evening paired with live music, and in Plano, Haggard Park is the go-to destination for just that. The Plano Community Band hosts a beloved summer concert series here, filling the historic gazebo with the sounds of show tunes, patriotic classics, and family-friendly favorites. These free performances draw a loyal crowd of locals who spread out picnic blankets and lawn chairs on the grass to enjoy the relaxed, come-as-you-are vibe.

But the music doesn't stop there. Throughout the season, Haggard Park also welcomes a variety of city-sponsored performances and cultural celebrations, often featuring local talent, student musicians, and themed concerts tied to Downtown Plano events. With the Interurban Railway Museum nearby and plenty of spots for preshow snacks or postconcert ice cream, it's a quintessential Plano experience you'll want to repeat all summer long.

901 E 15th St.
planoband.com

CELEBRATE PLANO'S CULTURE AND COMMUNITY AT LOCAL FESTIVALS

Plano comes alive year-round with festivals that celebrate its diversity, creativity, and community spirit. These festivals are a great way to experience the heart of the city through music, food, art, and shared moments under the Texas sky. Many are free to attend and take place in scenic outdoor settings like Oak Point Park.

Plano Balloon Festival

Held each September at Oak Point Park, this multiday event features early morning and evening hot-air balloon launches, a tethered balloon experience, live music, fireworks, and a kid zone.

2801 E Spring Creek Pkwy., 972-867-7566
planoballoonfest.org

Plano International Festival

Hosted at Haggard Park in October, this one-day celebration of global cultures includes live performances, world cuisine, multicultural booths, and a wellness fair.

901 E 15th St., 972-398-4200
planointernationalfestival.org

AsiaFest

This annual spring tradition presented by the Celebrating Asian American Heritage Foundation showcases Asian cultures through dance, music, food, and art.

901 E 15th St.
asianamericanheritage.org

Texas Forever Fest

Held each March in Downtown Plano, this one-day festival celebrates all things Texas: live music, local beer and barbecue, western-themed entertainment, and family fun.

Downtown Plano, 972-941-5613
plano.gov/2060/Texas-Forever-Fest

26

LAUGH OUT LOUD
AT MIC DROP COMEDY

For a high-energy night of laughs, head to Mic Drop Comedy in the Shops at Legacy North. This newer addition to Plano's entertainment scene offers stand-up shows from national headliners and up-and-coming comics in a lively, modern space. The vibe is social and upbeat—with shared tables and a packed room, it's not the spot for quiet conversation, but it's perfect for groups or a fun night out.

Surprisingly, the food here holds its own, with elevated bar bites and a solid cocktail menu featuring creative craft drinks. Shows are well paced, and the service is quick, even when the room is full. If you're craving comedy in a stylish setting with strong drinks and a big crowd, this is your place.

7301 Lone Star Dr., Ste. A-110, 469-440-9292
micdropcomedyplano.com

TIP

Come together in a group and get seated early. They club has a well-stocked bar you can order from while you wait for the show to start.

EXPERIENCE INCLUSIVE PERFORMANCES
AT NTPA REPERTORY

NTPA Repertory is one of Plano's most inclusive and inspiring arts organizations, offering professional-quality productions with a heart for community and accessibility. What makes it truly special is its dedication to showcasing actors of all ages, including performers with disabilities and members of the deaf community. Through thoughtful direction and creative storytelling, each production becomes a celebration of talent, inclusion, and the transformative power of the arts.

Audience members can expect moving, high-caliber performances in an intimate setting, while those who want to take the stage themselves are encouraged to join. NTPA offers opportunities for all experience levels, proving that great theater is made stronger by diversity and collaboration. It's a meaningful night out and one that often leaves a lasting impression.

6121 W Park Blvd., Ste. B216, 972-422-2575
ntparep.org

28

SKATE BACK IN TIME
AT THUNDERBIRD ROLLER RINK

Step inside Thunderbird Roller Rink and you're instantly transported to a retro dream—complete with a spinning glitter ball, vintage arcade games, and that unmistakable 1980s vibe that never goes out of style. This Plano institution has been around for decades, and it still delivers a friendly, affordable, and fun experience for all ages. Whether you're teaching your kids how to skate or reliving your roller rink glory days, it's a perfect way to spend an afternoon or evening with family and friends.

With budget-friendly prices, themed skate nights, and a welcoming staff, Thunderbird keeps things simple and fun. The snack bar won't break the bank, and skate rentals are available for quads, in-lines, and even walkers for little learners. It's no wonder this place still draws crowds after all these years.

3200 Thunderbird Ln., 972-422-4447
thunderbirdrink.com

TIP

Bring your skates to save a few bucks, wear tall socks, and show up early for the best parking.

GET MOVING

AT ACTIVATE—HIGH-TECH FUN FOR BIG KIDS AND ADULTS

Activate in Plano is part escape room, part video game, and all-out active fun. Designed for older kids, teens, and adults, this high-energy experience lets your group take on a series of interactive game rooms where speed, strategy, memory, and agility are all put to the test. Each room is unique, from laser mazes and color-matching walls to stealth challenges where you have to avoid a giant blinking eye (yes, really). It's a fast-paced environment where you're not just watching—you're in the action.

What makes Activate stand out? It's private to your group, with little to no waiting between games, and there's a spot to sit and recharge if you need a break. It's perfect for birthdays, friend groups, or even team-building outings. Just be sure to dress comfortably—you'll be running, jumping, dodging, and laughing your way through each challenge. After you've burned off some steam at Activate, drop by 151 Coffee for a huge choice of cold or nitro brew coffees, themed energy drinks, teas, smoothies, and a hot cider for the kids.

Activate
5013 W Plano Pkwy., Ste. 100, 469-209-6545
playactivate.com/plano

151 Coffee
1151 Preston Rd., 682-325-2124
151coffee.com

30

BOWL (AND EAT) IN STYLE
AT PLANO SUPER BOWL

Plano Super Bowl hits the sweet spot between classic fun and modern vibes. This locally loved bowling alley is clean, vibrant, and packed with personality, from its colorful decor to its surprisingly great Cajun-inspired kitchen. Whether you're there to throw strikes or just to sip a cold beer and cheer on your friends, it's a go-to spot for casual nights out, family fun, or even team events.

The lanes are well maintained, the music keeps the energy up, and the staff go out of their way to make sure everyone has a good time. There's also a pro shop for gear and upgrades, plus private event spaces for birthday parties or league nights. Even if you're not a bowler, the food, drinks, and upbeat atmosphere make it a fun night out in Plano.

2521 K Ave., 972-881-0242
planosuperbowl.com

TRY YOUR LUCK WITH BINGO IN PLANO

If you're looking for a fun, low-pressure way to socialize and unwind, bingo in Plano delivers a dose of friendly competition and community charm. Whether you're after high-stakes games with cash prizes or a laid-back session with friends, there are options for every kind of player. The best part? You don't need to be a pro. Just show up, grab a card, and enjoy the excitement as numbers are called.

Sam Johnson Recreation Center for Adults 50+

Daytime bingo games and social activities are designed for adults 50 and older. They're open to recreation center members and a great way to meet new friends.

401 W 16th St., 972-941-7155
plano.gov/1477/Sam-Johnson-Recreation-Center-for-Adults

East Plano Bingo

A dedicated bingo hall offering nightly games with cash prizes. It's fun, fast-paced, and supports local nonprofits.

2550 14th St., 972-578-9827
planobingo.com

Bingo Loco at Legacy Hall (21+)

A high-energy, DJ-fueled bingo party with confetti, themed music, and quirky prizes. It's bingo like you've never seen it before.

7800 Windrose Ave.
us.bingoloco.com/plano

SIP, PAINT, AND LAUGH
AT PAINTING WITH A TWIST

Painting with a Twist in Plano is the perfect mix of creativity and good company, whether you're planning a girls' night out or date night, or celebrating something special. The secret to their success? The instructors. Known for being fun, encouraging, and full of personality, they walk you through each step so even total beginners end up with a piece they're proud to hang at home.

Bring your favorite bottle of wine (it's BYOB), settle in with your group, and get ready for a low-pressure, laughter-filled experience. Each class features a different theme or painting, so you can come back again and again for something new. You might be surprised by how little artistic talent you need—and how much fun you'll have finding it. Just a short walk away, stop by Honeybird and pick up a cotton candy or s'more doughnut—it's just as pretty to look at as it is tasty to eat. Fuel up before you head over to paint.

Painting with a Twist
1713 Preston Rd., Ste. B, 469-814-0050
paintingwithatwist.com/studio/plano

Honeybird
1941 Preston Rd., Unit 1012, 469-464-4315
honeybirddfw.com

TIP

Go with an open mind! Even if you think you lack artistic talent, you'll be surprised to take home something you could hang on your wall.

32

ENJOY LIVE PERFORMANCES

AT THE COURTYARD THEATER

Located just steps from Downtown Plano's arts and dining scene, the Courtyard Theater is one of the city's most beloved performing arts venues. Built in 1938 as the Cox Theatre, this restored gem now hosts a vibrant mix of live performances, from community theater and student showcases to classical concerts and cultural festivals.

With just over 300 seats, the space offers an intimate experience where there's not a bad seat in the house.

It's home base for several local arts groups, including the Plano Symphony Orchestra's youth programs and North Texas Performing Arts. Whether you're catching a play, a choral concert, or a dance recital, the Courtyard blends history and creativity in one charming package. It's the kind of place where Plano's talent truly shines.

1509 H Ave., 972-941-5600
plano.gov/1067/Courtyard-Theater

TIP

There is a large parking lot behind the Courtyard Theater, accessible from G Avenue and 16th Street, with a quick walk to get to the theater.

33

DINE AND WATCH A MOVIE AT STUDIO MOVIE GRILL

If you're looking for an easy night out, Studio Movie Grill is a go-to in Plano. Enjoy the latest movies in a comfy recliner while your food and drinks are delivered right to your seat—just press the service button and relax. With reserved seating and friendly staff, it's a stress-free way to combine dinner, drinks, and a blockbuster in one stop.

Book your seats early, and aim for those in the middle (and back, of course!). You'll find out why if you are watching a movie during lunch or dinnertime. Get there early too. Arriving too late doesn't allow the kitchen time to cook your meal and get it delivered to your seat before or as the movie starts.

4721 W Park Blvd., Ste. 100, 469-405-8527
studiomoviegrill.com/locations/texas/plano

TIP

Catch a matinee before 4 p.m. for extra savings on the popular meal bundle.

34

GET CREATIVE
AT COLOR ME MINE PLANO

This was so fun!

Color Me Mine is a hands-on pottery painting studio where hidden artistic skills come to life. With shelves full of ready-to-paint pieces, from mugs and bowls to cute little astronaut sculptures, you'll find plenty of options for all ages and skill levels. You can walk in here without a reservation, so it's a perfect option for spontaneous artistic fun with family, friends, and kids of all ages.

We took a few hours here to get our designs just right and had a blast doing it.

After about two weeks, you return to pick up your glazed and fired masterpiece, and you'll be excited to see the final product. It's a relaxed, screen-free activity that's perfect for families or friend groups looking to do something creative together.

1713 Preston Rd., Ste. B, 214-258-5525
plano.colormemine.com

TIP

If you plan to stay a while, bring a cushion to sit on!

TEST YOUR BRAINPOWER WITH TRIVIA NIGHTS IN PLANO

Looking for a fun night out? Plano's trivia scene has you covered, with free games at local bars, breweries, and venues—plus prizes, themed nights, and plenty of laughs with friends.

Pluckers Wing Bar

It's one of the most popular trivia nights in Plano, held Wednesdays at 7:30 p.m. Great wings, cold drinks, and competitive teams make it a midweek favorite.

3316 Preston Rd., 972-599-9464
pluckers.com/locations-pages/plano

PinStack Plano

They offer themed trivia nights as part of their monthly "Party on the Patio" series, often tied to movies, holidays, or pop culture. It's held on the second Wednesday of each month from 7 to 9 p.m.

6205 Dallas Pkwy., 972-781-2695
pinstackbowl.com/locations/plano-texas

Dubs Tea N' Eats

It's a fun and casual spot for trivia every Wednesday from 6 to 9 p.m. Come for the tea flights and street-food-inspired bites and stay for the laughs and quirky team names.

3131 Custer Rd., Ste. 178, 972-985-2700
dubstea.net

Carpenter Skate Park

SPORTS AND RECREATION

35

PLAY ALL DAY

AT PLANO SPORTS AUTHORITY

Plano Sports Authority, better known as PSA, is where Plano families go to play, learn, and grow through sports. This community-based hub offers year-round indoor and outdoor facilities for basketball, soccer, volleyball, baseball, and flag and regular football.

PSA isn't just for team sports. It also hosts summer camps, drop-in programs, and classes for all skill levels, from beginners to serious young athletes. Need space for a birthday party or class? You can rent one of the versatile rooms. Parents will also appreciate the food court for mid-game snacks or waiting between activities.

With multiple locations and a welcoming, energetic atmosphere, PSA is a cornerstone of youth sports in Plano, where friendships form, confidence grows, and kids fall in love with being active.

6500 Preston Meadow Dr., 972-208-3803
psaplano.org

TIP

Before you arrive for a practice, a game, a camp, or a class, check with your team's coach or activity organizer which court and area you need to be at! You'd be surprised how much time it takes to find the right one when it's busy.

CRACK THE CODE IN A PLANO ESCAPE ROOM

Plano's escape rooms offer brain-boosting fun for all ages, whether you're solving a quick 10-minute challenge at Main Event or diving into immersive adventures at spots like North Texas Escape Room and Breakout Games. From kid-friendly quests to complex heists, it's a great way to mix up your routine with something memorable.

Main Event

3941 Central Expy., 972-881-8181
mainevent.com

North Texas Escape Rooms

8232 Preston Rd., Ste. 100, 469-609-0395
northtexasescaperooms.com

Breakout Games

2301 Central Expy., Ste. 285, 972-474-0111
breakoutgames.com

Red Door Escape Room

8103 Rasor Blvd., Ste. 100, 972-787-0085
reddoorescape.com

Quest Room

4320 K Ave., Ste. 309, 945-284-0084
questroom.com/dallas/locations/plano

MAKE A SPLASH
AT JACK CARTER POOL

When the Texas heat hits, Jack Carter Pool is the place to be. This city-run gem in the heart of Plano packs in all the thrills of a full-scale water park without the out-of-town drive or big-ticket prices. With two body slides, a dual-rider tube slide, a lazy river, and a deep-water pool featuring platform diving and a rock-climbing wall, there's something for every level of water lover.

Little ones will love the shaded splash play area, while older kids flock to the FlowRider surf simulator to test their skills. There's also a leisure pool for laid-back lounging and a concession stand for midday fuel. And better still? A day pass costs about the same as a cup of coffee, making it one of the most affordable summer outings in town.

Clean, safe, and packed with fun, Jack Carter is a Plano summer must.

2601 Pleasant Valley Dr., 972-208-8081
plano.gov/1456/Jack-Carter-Pool

37

SWIM ACROSS TEXAS
AT THE TEXAS POOL

Only in Plano can you swim across the state of Texas—literally. The Texas Pool, shaped like the Lone Star State and filled with saltwater, has been making summer memories since 1961. Listed on the National Register of Historic Places, this retro swim spot blends mid-century charm with deep community pride.

Our family loves it for the diving board, snack bar, and old-school vibe, but it's more than just a pool; it's a slice of local history. Many generations of Plano kids have grown up here, and it's still run by a nonprofit that hosts summer camps, swim lessons, holiday events, open swim days for all ages, and even events where you can swim with mermaids!

901 Springbrook Dr., 972-881-8393
texaspool.org

TIP

Memberships and day passes are available, and the Fourth of July party is always fun. Snap a photo from above if you can—you won't find another pool like it.

RELAX AND RECHARGE
AT GLENEAGLES COUNTRY CLUB

Gleneagles is one of Plano's most refined escapes. It's an upscale, members-only retreat in the heart of Plano. Nestled off West Park Boulevard, this private club features two championship golf courses, stunning event venues, and a dining experience that's equally suited for a laid-back lunch or a special celebration. Members often gather for business lunches, date nights, and milestone events in the club's polished yet comfortable atmosphere. Nonmembers can dine at the restaurant with beautiful views over the golf course and also book golf lessons.

Beyond golf, Gleneagles shines with top-tier tennis and pickleball facilities, including year-round leagues and clinics for all skill levels. The club's active social calendar includes seasonal dances, wine tastings, and kid-friendly programs like summer camps and holiday events. It's not just a place to play. It's a full-service community where members of all ages can feel right at home.

5401 W Park Blvd., 972-867-6666
invitedclubs.com/clubs/gleneagles-country-club

TIP

During weeknights, the club often has themed nights in the restaurant, so book your table ahead of time for a great view of the course.

HIT THE ICE
AT CHILDREN'S HEALTH STARCENTER PLANO

Even in the Texas heat, you'll find a cool escape at Children's Health StarCenter Plano. This premier ice facility is home to the Dallas Stars' youth hockey development programs, offering everything from beginner skating lessons to competitive hockey leagues. Whether your child dreams of playing center ice or just wants to try something new, this is the place to start.

The Learn to Play Hockey and Learn to Skate programs are thoughtfully designed for kids of all ages and skill levels. Coaches are supportive and experienced, creating a fun, confidence-building environment that introduces children to the fundamentals of ice sports. While hockey might not be as big in Texas as it is in other parts of the US, this facility is proof that the love of the game is growing strong in Plano.

4020 W Plano Pkwy., 214-975-7400
nhl.com/stars/starcenters/locations/plano

40

REACH NEW HEIGHTS
AT MOVEMENT PLANO

If you're looking for a fitness experience that goes beyond treadmills and weight racks, Movement Plano offers an energizing alternative. This indoor climbing gym has quickly become a community hub for climbers of all skill levels, from total beginners to seasoned pros. With bouldering, top rope, lead climbing, and auto belays, it's easy to find your groove whether you're climbing solo or with friends.

The atmosphere is warm, supportive, and surprisingly social. Many members say they came for the workout but stayed for the people. Movement isn't just about climbing—it also offers yoga classes, fitness training, and access to other locations nationwide, making the membership a great value. If you're curious, take advantage of the free intro class and see what makes this space so inviting. You might walk in for a workout and leave with a new favorite hobby and a few new friends.

525 Talbert Dr., 972-599-0865
movementgyms.com/plano

WORK OUT YOUR WAY AT PLANO'S TOP GYMS

Plano's fitness scene offers everything from luxury clubs with resort-style amenities to affordable gyms with 24/7 access. No matter your goals or schedule, there's a workout spot that fits your lifestyle.

Lifetime Fitness

7100 Preston Rd., 972-202-8130
lifetime.life/locations/tx/plano.html

Cowboys Fit

4817 W Park Blvd., 469-489-5901
cowboysfit.com/cowboysfit-plano

Crunch Fitness

1701 Preston Rd., 214-910-1660
crunch.com/locations/plano

EOS Fitness

3500 Preston Rd., Ste. 100., 214-764-1982
eosfitness.com/gym/plano-preston-rd-w-parker-rd

Plano Family YMCA

3300 McDermott Rd., 214-705-9459
ymcadallas.org/locations/plano

SERVE UP FUN
AT HIGH POINT TENNIS CENTER

High Point Tennis Center has long been a local favorite for tennis enthusiasts, and recent renovations have only elevated the experience. With resurfaced outdoor courts, expanded programming, and a welcoming atmosphere, it's one of the best public facilities in North Texas for both tennis and pickleball.

Pickleball is quickly gaining momentum here, with dedicated courts, leagues, and classes available throughout the week. First-timers can borrow demo paddles, and the cost to play is remarkably low, just a few dollars per session. Court reservations are required and easy to make online with a City of Plano account. Whether you're rallying on the tennis court or diving into a fast-paced pickleball match, High Point offers something for every skill level and age.

421 W Spring Creek Pkwy., 972-941-7170
highpointtennis.com

TIP

Take note of the day and time when booking opens and closes for each season for the most availability in classes.

42

PLAY PICKLEBALL AND CONNECT
AT CHASE OAKS CHURCH

Pickleball has exploded in popularity, and Chase Oaks Church–Legacy Campus is leading the way in Plano with some of the most accessible and well-kept outdoor courts around. Open to the public and completely free to use, the space includes multiple professional-grade courts with permanent nets, clear boundary lines, and shaded seating for spectators and players alike.

The vibe is friendly and inclusive, perfect for both beginners and seasoned players. Clinics and casual tournaments are held regularly, often in partnership with Local Good Coffee, the on-site café that adds a social touch to your visit. Whether you're here to rally or gather with family at a community event featuring music, games, bounce houses, and food, the church has created a welcoming place that blends play and community.

201 Legacy Dr., 469-925-0599
localgoodcoffee.com

TIP

Visit in the early morning or evening to avoid the heat, and check the website for open play hours and court rules.

SKATE THE RAMPS
AT CARPENTER PARK SKATE PARK

If you've got a skateboard (or a scooter or BMX bike) and a sense of adventure, Carpenter Park Skate Park is calling your name. Tucked inside one of Plano's largest and most active parks, this outdoor concrete park is a local favorite for skaters of all ages. Whether you're a beginner learning how to drop in or a seasoned rider mastering technical tricks, the mix of bowls, ramps, ledges, and rails offers a little something for everyone.

The best part? It's completely free and open daily from sunrise to 11 p.m., with stadium-style lights that keep the fun going after dark.

It's an unsupervised outdoor spot. You'll need to bring your own board, scooter, or BMX bike with you. The atmosphere is friendly, and on weekends you'll often spot local talent showing off some serious skills.

6701 Coit Rd., 972-208-8087
plano.gov/1543/Skate-Park-at-Carpenter-Park

TIP

Pads and helmets are strongly encouraged. Even the pros wear them. And if you're new to skating, try visiting on weekday mornings when the park is less crowded.

JOIN THE FUN WITH ADAPTED RECREATION
AT PLANO PARKS AND RECREATION

Plano Parks and Recreation's Adapted Recreation program is a hidden gem for families with children and teens who have special needs. Designed specifically for individuals with intellectual or physical disabilities, these programs offer a supportive, welcoming environment where every participant feels seen, respected, and valued. The staff at the recreation centers are more than just instructors. They're mentors who build real connections with the kids they serve.

For youth ages 11 to 17, the Adapted Recreation classes are a great way to build confidence, learn new skills, and make lasting friendships. From social clubs and sports to art and fitness, there's something to fit a wide range of interests and abilities. Parents often notice not just growth in skills but a real sense of belonging.

Classes at Carpenter Park Recreation Center
and other City of Plano recreation facilities
972-208-8087
plano.gov/882/Adapted-Recreation

TIP

These programs fill up fast, so check out the schedule early and register online.

45

TEST YOUR SKILLS
AT GO APE ZIPLINE & ADVENTURE PARK

If you're craving an outdoor adventure that pushes you out of your comfort zone, Go Ape at Oak Point Park delivers. This high-flying treetop course winds through the lush canopy of Plano's largest nature preserve, offering zip lines, Tarzan swings, and wobbly bridges that challenge your balance, courage, and maybe even your fear of heights. It's an unforgettable experience for thrill seekers and families with teens looking to do something different.

Expect about two to three hours of climbing, swinging, and soaring. The staff are friendly and safety-focused, so even first-timers feel confident navigating the course. While younger kids can't participate in the full adventure, there's plenty of room nearby for them to cheer from below or explore the trails while they wait. Be sure to read the rules online before you go, and book your date and time slot to ensure you can enjoy it on your timeline without waiting.

5901 Los Rios Blvd., 800-971-8271
goape.com/location/texas-plano

TIP

Closed-toe shoes are a must, and reservations are recommended, especially on weekends.

PLAY A ROUND
AT SHAWNEE PARK DISC GOLF COURSE

Tucked away in a scenic corner of East Plano, Shawnee Park is a local favorite for disc golf enthusiasts. This tree-lined nine-hole course blends open fairways with strategic obstacles, making it a great choice for both beginners and more seasoned players. Whether you're working on distance or just looking for a casual weekend round with friends, it offers a relaxed, welcoming vibe.

The park itself is beautiful, with a mix of concrete and dirt trails, a creek that's perfect for cooling off postgame, and plenty of green space to let the kids run free. It's also a great place for walking, running, or simply enjoying nature. It's completely free to play. If you're looking for other players to meet there, there are online groups you can join. Bring your discs, grab some water, and enjoy one of Plano's most underrated outdoor gems.

3380 Sherwood Dr., 972-941-7275
plano.gov/1497/Shawnee-Park-Disc-Golf-Course

JOIN THE CRAZE
AT PICKLEBALL KINGDOM PLANO

Pickleball has officially taken over DFW, and Pickleball Kingdom Plano is leading the charge in the heart of the city. This clean, modern facility is fully dedicated to the sport, with courts available for open play, beginner classes, and competitive matches. Whether you're just learning the basics or already addicted to the game, this is your new home court.

The atmosphere is welcoming, and there are an abundance of courts to use, lessons for beginners, and membership options that make it easy to play regularly. Drop-in sessions are perfect for testing the waters or meeting other players, and the staff makes sure everyone, from first-timers to seasoned picklers, feels comfortable and ready to play.

Conveniently located in Central Plano, it's the perfect spot to get active, have fun, and be part of a fast-growing, friendly community.

1301 Custer Rd., Ste. 200, 469-969-0000
pickleballkingdom.com/plano

WANDER AND RECHARGE

AT OAK POINT PARK AND NATURE PRESERVE

Oak Point Park and Nature Preserve offers one of the most peaceful escapes in Plano, without ever leaving the city. Spanning over 800 acres, this expansive green space features a mix of wide-open fields, wooded trails, scenic creeks, and a tranquil lake perfect for kayaking. Whether you're skimming rocks by the water's edge or taking in golden-hour views, it's a breath of fresh air just minutes from home.

The trail system includes both soft-surface paths and paved routes, making it ideal for walking, jogging, or biking. And don't worry; no hiking boots are required. The mostly flat terrain and well-marked trails welcome all ages and abilities. Whether you're looking for solitude, wildlife spotting, or just a nature walk with the kids, Oak Point makes it easy to get outside and reconnect with nature.

5901 Los Rios Blvd., 972-941-7250
plano.gov/1476/Oak-Point-Park-Nature-Preserve

49

RUN THE TRAILS
AT ARBOR HILLS NATURE PRESERVE

Arbor Hills Nature Preserve is where Plano's natural beauty truly comes to life. With a mix of paved and unpaved trails winding through 200 acres of wooded hills, open fields, and creeks, it's a favorite for walkers, runners, and nature lovers alike. The trails are well marked, dog friendly, and offer just enough elevation to get your heart pumping, so don't be surprised if your calves feel the workout the next day.

One of the highlights is the scenic lookout tower, where you can take in sweeping views of the surrounding landscape. There's also a playground for kids, a covered pavilion for picnics, and plenty of shaded spots to rest. Whether you're training for a 10K or just enjoying a peaceful stroll, Arbor Hills offers the perfect blend of challenge and serenity and a fun place for kids and adults alike. Be sure to check the trail you choose, as one of them is significantly longer than the other.

6701 W Parker Rd., 972-941-7250
plano.gov/1397/Arbor-Hills-Nature-Preserve

TIP

Arrive early to beat the crowds, especially on weekends. The parking lot fills up fast.

50

SWIM LAPS OR MAKE A SPLASH

AT OAK POINT RECREATION CENTER

Whether you're training for a triathlon or just looking to get your laps in, Oak Point Recreation Center is Plano's go-to spot for serious swimmers. The centerpiece? A massive Olympic-sized indoor pool with 16 dedicated lap lanes. The space is bright, clean, and often filled with motivated swimmers slicing through the water. It's one of the best year-round spots to keep up your cardio or perfect your stroke.

But it's not just for athletes. Families love the newly renovated outdoor area, complete with a splash pad and a wave pool that adds some serious fun to sunny days. For little ones, Tots Splash Time offers a safe and playful water experience every Monday, Wednesday, and Friday, ideal for introducing young kids to the water in a calm environment.

6000 Jupiter Rd., 972-941-7540
plano.gov/1465/Oak-Point-Recreation-Center

TIP

Early mornings are perfect for lap swimmers who want a quiet pool. Check the center's schedule for lane availability before heading over.

51

RIDE THE CHISHOLM TRAIL BIKE PATH

The Chisholm Trail Bike Path is a favorite for locals who want to enjoy nature without ever leaving the city. Stretching from Harrington Park near Downtown Plano to Legacy Drive, this scenic multiuse trail weaves through wooded greenbelts and quiet neighborhoods, and along meandering creeks. It's a peaceful, shaded route perfect for biking, jogging, or leisurely walks with the family.

With several underpasses and crosswalks, the trail offers a surprisingly uninterrupted journey through the heart of Plano. You'll pass playgrounds, open fields, and even a few hidden picnic spots along the way. Whether you're commuting on two wheels or just getting some fresh air, the Chisholm Trail is a go-to escape that feels worlds away from busy streets.

Starts at Harrington Park (401 W 16th St.) and ends near Legacy Dr.
972-941-7250
plano.gov/1451/Chisholm-Trail

TIP

If you get lost, look for the marker signs to indicate your location in case you need to call a friend to find you or 911.

TAKE YOUR PUP
TO WINDHAVEN MEADOWS DOG PARK

If your dog needs room to run, Windhaven Meadows Dog Park is a must-visit. Spanning five acres, this off-leash park features dedicated areas for both small and large dogs, so pups can play safely with dogs their size. Agility equipment adds extra fun and challenge, while shaded seating and water stations keep everyone cool and hydrated.

Located within the larger Windhaven Meadows Park, it's easy to make a day of it. Bring the kids to the inclusive playground, enjoy a walk on the nearby trails, or just relax and watch the dogs have the time of their lives. It's one of Plano's most inviting outdoor spaces for pets and their people.

5400 Windhaven Pkwy., 972-941-7250
plano.gov/1515/Dog-Park-at-Windhaven-Meadows-Park

TIP

It's a wide-open space with some shade. Be sure to wear a hat and ensure your dog is well hydrated if you're planning to be out for a longer walk during the daytime.

53

EXPERIENCE THE MAGIC
OF PLANO'S HOLIDAY PARADE AND TREE LIGHTINGS

When the holiday season rolls around, Plano transforms into a festive wonderland filled with twinkling lights, community cheer, and timeless traditions. One of the most anticipated events of the year is the annual Plano Lions Christmas Parade, where local schools, businesses, and community groups parade through the streets with floats, marching bands, dancers, and even a visit from Santa himself. It's a heartwarming hometown celebration that brings families together and kicks off the season in true Plano style.

Just a short walk away in historic Downtown Plano, Haggard Park hosts the city's official Tree Lighting Ceremony, complete with carolers, hot chocolate, family-friendly activities, and holiday photo ops. Kids can meet Santa, explore local vendor booths, and watch the park light up with thousands of sparkling bulbs. These events are more than just photo ops; they're part of the spirit that makes Plano feel like home during the holidays.

Haggard Park, 901 E 15th St., 972-941-5600

ESCAPE TO THE ZEN POOL AND BAR
AT RENAISSANCE DALLAS AT PLANO LEGACY WEST

For a true retreat in the middle of Plano, head to the Zen Pool and Bar at the Renaissance Dallas at Plano Legacy West Hotel. This rooftop oasis is open to hotel guests and features a sparkling pool, chic cabanas, and sweeping city views, perfect for lounging or enjoying with some fun friends.

Enjoy a cocktail and the resort-style atmosphere with fun playlists and great attentive service at the poolside. We love to book a night and enjoy the sunset with a view. You can also book a day pass or a cabana, too.

6007 Legacy Dr., 469-925-1800

TIP

Legacy West also offers a variety of great restaurants for the perfect way to wrap up your day at the Zen Pool and Bar.

Heritage Farmstead Museum
Credit Jennifer Shertzer

CULTURE AND HISTORY

STEP BACK IN TIME
AT THE HERITAGE FARMSTEAD MUSEUM

Plano may be a booming modern city now, but at the Heritage Farmstead Museum, you can experience life as it once was: unhurried, hardworking, and rooted in the land. This 4.5-acre living history site is one of the best-preserved examples of North Texas prairie life, complete with barns, a blacksmith shop, livestock pens, and a one-room schoolhouse.

You can easily walk around with strollers or wheelchairs as the farm grounds are ADA compliant with decomposed granite walkways. In their store, you can purchase feed for the free-range chickens. If you go at the right time, you can also ride the wagon to tour the farm.

Kids can explore farm life through fun-filled summer camps, learning about animals, crops, and the rhythm of rural living. And if you're planning a wedding, party, or special gathering, this unique space is available for private rentals with a beautifully rustic backdrop.

1900 W 15th St., 972-881-0140
heritagefarmstead.org

TIP

Don't miss the antique tractor display, the donkey and goats, or the friendly chickens near the coop. They're all kid magnets!

TOUR PLANO'S OLDEST HOME:
THE FARRELL-WILSON HOUSE

At the heart of the Heritage Farmstead Museum stands the Farrell-Wilson House, a beautifully preserved Queen Anne–style Victorian home that dates back to 1891. Recognized as the oldest standing house in Plano, it offers a vivid window into life on the Texas prairie during the late 19th and early 20th centuries.

Built by Hunter Farrell and later managed by his daughter, Ammie Wilson, this four-bedroom home was part of a thriving 360-acre farm. Wilson became one of the first women in the region to own and operate a large farm, raising sheep and cattle long before it was common for women to lead in the agricultural sector. Today, the home is fully furnished with period pieces, providing visitors with a genuine sense of the era's lifestyle, from the parlor to the pantry.

1900 W 15th St. (on the grounds of the Heritage Farmstead Museum)
972-881-0140
heritagefarmstead.org

TIP

Be sure to take the guided tour, which is included with museum admission. Docents often share personal stories and surprising details you won't find on the signs.

EXPLORE 150 YEARS OF BLACK HISTORY

IN THE DOUGLASS COMMUNITY

For over 150 years, the Douglass Community has been a cornerstone of black history in Plano. Founded by formerly enslaved families after emancipation, it grew into a vibrant neighborhood with its shops, churches, and schools. During segregation, residents supported each other and created a world of their own, which longtime resident Dollie Thomas calls “a thriving community within a community.”

Walk back in time along I Avenue, once the main street of the Douglass Community, where black-owned restaurants, barbershops, beauty salons, and small businesses formed a village during segregation. Neighbors sold treats from kitchen doors, children stopped at the Blue Room after church, and Shiloh Church was their place of worship.

Nearby, the Douglass Community mural tells this powerful story through art, and just down the street, the Davis and Old City Cemeteries quietly reflect a legacy of segregation, and the progress since.

900 13th St., 469-863-7226
planoafricanamericanmuseum.org

CONNECT WITH THE ROOTS OF HAGGARD FARM

Before tech campuses and tollways defined Plano's skyline, the land was farmland, and much of it belonged to the Haggard family. One of Plano's earliest settler families, the Haggards arrived from Kentucky in the mid-1800s and helped shape the community for generations. C. S. Haggard famously brought a massive male donkey, nicknamed Mammoth Jack, with him in a covered wagon. That Jack sired a line of mules that earned Plano the title "Mule Capital of the World" by the 1860s.

Today, the legacy of Haggard Farm lives on at the southwest corner of Park and Coit, where the family still runs a working farm. Though much of Plano has changed, this peaceful corner serves as a reminder of the city's agricultural roots. Red barns, grazing livestock, and hay bales offer a glimpse of what the area once looked like, long before the suburbs arrived. The Haggard family often opens up their party barn for public events and private parties. Inside the barn, you'll find tons of historical farm artifacts and photos of the family and their farm staff from years past.

Southwest corner of Park Blvd. and Coit Rd.

TIP

It is not open for tours, but you can drive by the property or spot the Haggard name on streets, libraries, and civic buildings all over Plano. Look out for horses and llamas, which were brought in to guard against coyotes.

STROLL THROUGH TIME
IN HISTORIC DOWNTOWN PLANO

Look closely as you wander through historic Downtown Plano—many of the red-brick buildings carry plaques and signage telling the stories of what once stood there. Step inside and you might find original features like exposed brick walls, especially at Event1013, a former department store turned event venue.

This walkable district blends small-town roots with big-city energy. Once a stop on the Texas Electric Railway, it's now home to local boutiques, coffee shops, galleries, and live music venues. At McCall Plaza and Haggard Park, you'll often find concerts, festivals, and markets that bring the community together. The DART Rail runs right through downtown, connecting Plano to the rest of the Dallas–Fort Worth area and making it an easy destination for a day trip or night out.

Centered around 15th St. and Avenue K
972-941-7155 (for Downtown Plano Arts District events)
visitdowntownplano.com

TIP

Visit the Interurban Railway Museum to step aboard a restored railcar, and don't miss the public art scattered throughout alleys and corners; you'll be surprised by what you find.

STEP INSIDE PLANO'S FIRST HIGH SCHOOL AT THE COX BUILDING

Before it became a Plano ISD administration building, the Cox Building opened its doors in 1924 as Plano High School. Nearly a century later, this historic structure still serves education, now as a quiet monument to how far the district has come.

On the second floor, the Classroom Museum re-creates a vintage schoolroom and showcases a timeline of Plano ISD's growth. You'll find old-fashioned desks, school memorabilia, and historic posters that chart the district's evolution from a small-town schoolhouse to one of the most respected systems in Texas. It's a nostalgic and inspiring stop for anyone with ties to Plano schools or a love for educational history.

Stop by the Courtyard Theater to envision the high school's gymnasium before it was converted into what you see today.

1517 H Ave.
469-752-8150 (Plano ISD Administration)

TIP

Call ahead to see if the museum is open or available by request.

PEEK INSIDE A HIDDEN VAULT AT THE A. R. SCHELL BUILDING

Not every historic gem in Downtown Plano is out in the open. At 1001 East 15th Street, the A. R. Schell Insurance Building quietly holds one of the city's most unexpected relics: a century-old bank vault, still tucked inside what is now a modern office space.

A. R. Schell was a civic leader and insurance agent in early 20th-century Plano. His building once housed a bank and later became his namesake insurance office. If you get the chance to step inside, you'll find the original walk-in vault still intact, complete with heavy steel doors and a timeworn charm that hints at its past life.

It's a rare example of how Plano's earliest commercial buildings blended function and fortitude. Today, the building isn't a museum, but if you catch it during an open house or community event, it's a surprising and memorable piece of Plano history.

1001 E 15th St., Ste. 100

VISIT THE PLANO AFRICAN AMERICAN MUSEUM

Set in the heart of the Douglass Community, the Plano African American Museum honors more than 150 years of local black history, culture, and achievement. Housed in the historic Frederick Douglass School building, the museum tells the story of a community that created its schools, churches, and businesses in the face of segregation and helped shape Plano's path toward integration.

The museum first took root online during the COVID-19 shutdown, as volunteers began collecting oral histories, photographs, and records to preserve the stories of Plano's black families. Over the past three years, they've grown that effort into a physical space. With the help of community leaders and local support, the museum now includes curated artifacts and interpretive displays that bring these stories to life.

While still expanding, it remains a powerful place to connect with Plano's past and the people who shaped it. As board members T. J. Johnson and Willie Rivers say, "Touch the wood, see what we're building, and be part of preserving this history."

900 13th St., 469-863-7226
planoafricanamericanmuseum.org

HONOR LOCAL HEROES
AT MEMORIAL PARK

Just off Spring Creek Parkway, Memorial Park is one of Plano's most serene and heartfelt spaces. This peaceful green space is dedicated to the men and women from Plano who served in the US Armed Forces. At its center stands the Veterans Memorial, a granite monument engraved with the names of local heroes who gave their lives in service, each one representing a powerful story of sacrifice.

Surrounded by shady trees, walking trails, and benches, the park invites quiet reflection. It's not a large or flashy memorial, but its simplicity is what makes it so moving. The city holds remembrance ceremonies here throughout the year, including on Veterans Day and Memorial Day, bringing the community together to honor the legacy of those who served.

2101 Bay Hill Dr.
plano.gov/1475/Memorial-Park

TIP

Join residents, veterans, and council members each year who gather for a Memorial Day event to remember.

64

WALK THE CATTLE TRAIL
AT BACCUS PLAZA

Right in the middle of the Shops at Legacy East, surrounded by restaurants, hotels, and high-rises, you'll stumble upon something truly unexpected: a herd of longhorns and three cowboys charging across a grassy plaza. *Trails in Legacy* is a stunning bronze sculpture installation by Texas artist Robert Summers that pays tribute to the historic Shawnee Trail, which once ran through this area.

The detail in the statues is incredible, and each of the three cowboys represents a different part of Texas history, including a black cowboy and a vaquero, honoring the real diversity of the Old West. Kids love weaving between the 19 bronze steers, and grown-ups can't help but take a photo or two. It's just that impressive.

Baccus Plaza at the Shops at Legacy, just west of Bishop Rd.
469-467-9995
shopsatlegacy.com

TIP

Head over just before sunset for beautiful lighting and fewer crowds. And don't forget to look around; Baccus Plaza is surrounded by great spots for dinner or a treat.

RIDE THROUGH TIME
AT THE INTERURBAN RAILWAY MUSEUM

Step into Plano's early 20th-century past at the Interurban Railway Museum, right at the corner of Haggard Park in Downtown Plano. This free, family-friendly museum shares the story of the Texas Electric Railway (which once connected Plano to Dallas and beyond), long before the days of cars and highways.

Inside, you'll find exhibits on Plano's railroad history, electricity, and the people who made the railway run. It's especially fun for kids, with hands-on activities and a Story Time with Motorman Harold every Friday at 11 a.m. It's one of those hidden gems that surprises visitors with so much to see and learn.

Meeting the volunteers who serve here, who love to share their stories of Plano in the past, is worth a visit for this alone.

901 E 15th St., 972-941-2117
interurbanrailwaymuseum.org

TIP

Start here, then walk the rest of Downtown Plano; many of the historic buildings were built during the Interurban's heyday.

CLIMB ABOARD HISTORIC CAR 360
IN DOWNTOWN PLANO

One of the most unique features at the Interurban Railway Museum is Car #360, a restored electric railcar that once carried passengers and the mail between cities in North Texas. Known as a Railway Post Office car, it's one of the few still in existence and lets you see how mail was sorted and delivered on the go.

Step inside, and you'll get a feel for what travel was like in the early 1900s, complete with wooden benches, old signage, and working mail slots. Kids love exploring the compartments and imagining what it was like to ride this car decades ago. It's the kind of place where history feels tangible—and where you're encouraged to touch, learn, and explore.

901 E 15th St. (on museum grounds), 972-941-2117
interurbanrailwaymuseum.org

TIP

Access to the car is included with admission to the museum (which is free), but it's best to visit during staffed hours so you can go inside.

MEET THE IRON HORSE
OF DOWNTOWN PLANO

Standing guard near the DART station, a striking metallic horse catches everyone's eye. Created by artist Tom Askman, this life-sized industrial stallion pays homage to the transition from a quiet farming town into a bustling railway stop.

The stylized life-sized sculpture was commissioned by Dallas Area Rapid Transit (DART) and reflects the "iron horse" trains that once passed through Plano on the Interurban Line.

It's a fun and quirky photo op—a life-size, industrial-looking horse sculpture with real historical roots. If you're lucky, you may spot a crocheted bonnet that a resident has added to the iron horse from time to time, and if you look closely, you'll see bronze flies on the body of the horse—a key detail that brings the sculpture to life.

Near DART Rail Station, 15th St. and K Ave.

TIP

Pair your visit with a walk through Downtown Plano or a stop at Haggard Park. It's all connected to the same chapter of Plano's agricultural past.

REFLECT ON THE PAST
AT OLD CITY AND DAVIS CEMETERY

Head to 18th Street to find one of Plano's oldest and most historic sites: Old City and Davis Cemetery. Though they sit side by side today, these two cemeteries were once separated by a physical fence, one designated for white residents, the other for black residents during the time of segregation.

Old City Cemetery is the final resting place of many of Plano's founding families, with headstones dating back to the 1880s. Davis Cemetery, just next to it, holds generations of black families, including leaders of the Douglass Community. The fence that once divided them has been removed, and the two sites are now unified by shared care and recognition.

18th St., between G Ave. and Jupiter Rd.
972-941-7155 (City of Plano Parks and Cemeteries)
plano.gov

TIP

When you visit, consider the impact of L. A. Davis, who arrived in Plano as a sharecropper and built wealth through real estate and stocks. In 1945, he bought the plot of vacant land and established the L. A. Davis Cemetery, reserved as a resting place for African Americans.

69

DISCOVER THE MYSTERY
OF THE COLLINWOOD HOUSE

Is it the oldest house in Plano? That depends on whom you ask. While the Farrell-Wilson House holds the official title, many believe the Collinwood House, dating back to around 1861, may be older. This modest farmhouse, now located on Haggard Farm land just off Parkwood Boulevard in West Plano, has quietly witnessed more than 160 years of local history.

Once part of a working homestead, the Collinwood House has been moved, preserved, and fought for by community members who value its connection to Plano's rural roots. Though it's not open to the public, its simple wooden frame and weathered charm tell a story of early settlers, hard work, and changing times on the Texas prairie.

On Haggard Farm land near Parkwood Blvd.
and Windhaven Pkwy.

TIP

While you can't tour the inside, it's visible from the road. Swing by when you're near Parkwood and Windhaven to glimpse this hidden piece of Plano's past.

CHECK OUT

THE PLANO ART WALK

Want to explore Plano's history and creativity on your schedule? The Plano Art Walk is a self-guided walking tour that weaves through Downtown Plano, connecting public art, historic landmarks, sculptures, and cultural spots like the ArtCentre of Plano and the Interurban Railway Museum. Created by a passionate group of Leadership Plano alumni, this online resource is free to access and download.

Using a mobile-friendly map from planoartwalk.com, you can choose from a "Walk with Kids" or "Walk with Adults" at your own pace while discovering murals, sculpture installations, and surprising stories along the way. Each stop comes with descriptions and context, making it easy to walk and learn about Plano's artistic and historic roots at the same time.

Various stops around Downtown Plano
planoartwalk.com

TIP

Start near Haggard Park and circle back for lunch or coffee. Many of the best stops are within just a few blocks of each other.

SEE WHAT'S ON THE WALLS

AT ARTCENTRE OF PLANO AND THE COURTYARD THEATER

If you love discovering art in intimate, unexpected places, Downtown Plano has two hidden gems you won't want to miss. Housed in the beautifully restored Saigling House, the ArtCentre of Plano offers a cozy gallery space that regularly rotates exhibitions from local artists, photographers, and regional creatives. The setting—complete with creaky wood floors and views of Haggard Park—adds just the right touch of charm.

Just around the corner, the Courtyard Theater is best known for its stage productions, but the lobby often doubles as a gallery space. You'll find community art shows, student exhibits, and special installations that change throughout the year. Together, these two venues make a great hub for local art in Plano.

ArtCentre of Plano
902 E 16th St., 972-423-7809
artcentreofplano.org

Courtyard Theater
1509 H Ave., 972-941-5600
plano.gov

TIP

Time your visit during a Downtown Plano art or music event, as many exhibits are open late during festivals and performances.

VISIT THE EWING MANSION AT SOUTHFORK RANCH

If you grew up watching *Dallas*, you already know Southfork Ranch, the grand estate of the oil-rich, drama-filled Ewing family. What you may not know is that the famous Ewing Mansion is just minutes from Plano, in the town of Parker. Whether you're a fan of the show or just curious about this piece of pop-culture history, Southfork offers a surprisingly fun and nostalgic visit.

You can take a guided tour of the mansion, walk through the same rooms where J. R. schemed and Sue Ellen brooded, and explore behind-the-scenes memorabilia from the series. The ranch grounds are also home to a museum, stables, and an event space. Even if you weren't a viewer, it's still worth a trip for the Texas-sized scenery and the chance to say you stood on the most famous front porch in TV history.

3700 Hogge Rd., Parker, 972-442-7800
southforkranch.com

TIP

Make a reservation for a mansion tour, especially during weekends or event days. It's a great place to bring out-of-town guests for a dose of Texas flair.

73

FIND HISTORY BENEATH THE SURFACE
AT THE PLANO MASONIC LODGE

Just off 15th Street, the Plano Masonic Lodge #768 sits quietly on J Avenue—easy to miss unless you know what to look for. But this unassuming brick building has deep roots. Built in the early 1900s, it once housed the Moore Hotel, which served travelers arriving by rail. Over the years, it became a gathering place for members of the Masonic Order, one of the city's earliest fraternal organizations.

A Texas historical marker outside tells the story of its evolution, and if you catch it during a Downtown Plano walking tour or open house, you may get a peek inside. Though the lodge is still active and not regularly open to the public, it stands as a reminder of how transportation, civic life, and brotherhood shaped early Plano.

1414 J Ave., 972-905-1714

TIP

Look for the building just a block off 15th Street. It's a quick but meaningful stop during a stroll through the Downtown Arts District.

SEE WHAT'S NEW
AT THE ART GALLERY AT COLLIN COLLEGE

Located on the Spring Creek Campus of Collin College, the Arts Gallery is one of Plano's best-kept cultural secrets. Free and open to the public, this professional-level gallery features rotating exhibitions from local, regional, and nationally recognized artists, as well as standout student showcases throughout the year. You'll find a wide range of media, from painting and photography to sculpture and digital installations, all thoughtfully curated by the college's Visual Arts faculty.

Head inside Fannin Hall. This hidden gem offers a quiet, reflective space that surprises first-time visitors with the caliber of work on display. Many exhibits include opening receptions or artist talks, giving guests a chance to engage more deeply with the art and the artists behind it.

2800 E Spring Creek Pkwy. (Fannin Hall), 972-881-5873
collin.edu/department/artsgallery

TIP

Parking is free and easy, and the gallery is typically open Monday through Friday when classes are in session. Check the calendar online before you go.

DISCOVER A HIDDEN GEM IN DOWNTOWN PLANO:

MUSEUM OF CONTEMPORARY VISUAL ART (MOCVA)

Tucked into the heart of downtown, the Museum of Contemporary Visual Art (MOCVA) is quickly becoming Plano's hidden gem for art lovers and the art-curious alike. This museum brings together global and local artists, with thought-provoking exhibits that reveal the stories and inspiration behind each piece. You'll find bold paintings, immersive installations, and sculptures that invite you to linger, look closer, and even start a conversation.

One of the best parts of visiting MOCVA is the chance to mix and mingle with the artists themselves during exhibit openings, workshops, or talks.

1201 E 15th St., 214-773-5696
mocva.org

TIP

Be sure to chat with the museum curators and staff about the stories behind the art and the artists they feature.

CONNECT WITH LOCAL CREATIVES
AT TEN 20 ART GALLERY

If you're looking to tap into Plano's thriving art scene, Ten 20 Art Gallery is a must-visit. This welcoming space in Downtown Plano brings together local artists and art lovers, showcasing original paintings, photography, and mixed media in an intimate gallery setting. You'll find exhibits that change regularly.

Ten 20 Art Gallery is more than just a place to look at art. It's a place to connect. Meet the artists, ask about their inspiration, and even take home a favorite piece. With open hours from noon to 8 p.m. Thursday through Saturday, and noon to 4 p.m. on Sunday, it's easy to stop by after lunch or as part of a weekend stroll.

1001 14th St., Ste. 200

TIP

Check the event calendar for artist receptions or themed show openings—these are the best times to mix, mingle, and experience Plano's creative energy firsthand.

DISCOVER THE GENEALOGY CENTER
AT PLANO PUBLIC LIBRARY

At the Genealogy Center inside Haggard Library, you can uncover Plano's past one story at a time. This research hub houses local archives, historic newspapers, and family records from Collin County and beyond. Visitors can view old city maps, explore digitized *Plano Star Courier* issues, and scan documents to take home.

While materials can't be checked out, on-site access to Ancestry.com and other genealogy databases makes research simple. Librarians offer appointments by email, and monthly workshops—both online and in person—help beginners and experts alike.

Don't miss Collin County Images, a digital collection of journals, photos, and family histories from Plano's earliest settlers.

2501 Coit Rd., 972-769-4200
genealogy@plano.gov
planolibrary.org

Learning Express Toys & Gifts

SHOPPING AND FASHION

STROLL INTO LYLA'S CLOTHING & GIFTS FOR LOCAL FLAIR AND FAB FINDS

In the heart of historic Downtown Plano, Lyla's is a colorful, can't-miss boutique brimming with charm. This family-owned gem offers a playful mix of women's clothing, home decor, and giftable goodies with a distinct Texas twist. Think: graphic tees, cheeky mugs, and artful pieces that show off your Plano pride.

The shelves are stocked with seasonal items, candles, accessories, and quirky treasures you didn't know you needed until you saw them.

Shopping from afar? Lyla's also offers a robust online store so you can bring a little bit of Downtown Plano home, no matter where you are.

1024 E 15th St., 214-907-6239
lylasclothing.com

TIP

If you are looking to match your gift choice with your friends' passions, you'll be sure to find it here!

TREASURE HUNT FOR A CAUSE
AT HOPE'S DOOR RESALE STORE

For thrift lovers with a purpose, Hope's Door New Beginning Center Resale Store in Plano is a hidden gem worth discovering and revisiting often. Recently relocated to a bright and welcoming corner space (formerly the Texas DPS office), the store feels more like a cozy boutique than your typical thrift shop. No musty smells, no overwhelming clutter—just clean, organized racks and inviting displays.

You'll find gently used, sometimes brand-new clothing, handbags, shoes, children's books, jewelry, and unique home decor. Prices are wallet friendly, and the experience is always pleasant, thanks in large part to the kind-hearted staff whose warm smiles make regulars feel right at home.

Even better? Every dollar spent helps fund Hope's Door New Beginning Center, which supports survivors of domestic violence. Shopping here means walking out with something wonderful—and knowing you've helped someone in the process.

2109 W Parker Rd., Ste. 224, 972-769-0610
hdnbc.org/resale-store

80

DIG FOR BARGAINS
AT PLAZA THRIFT

If you love the thrill of the hunt, Plaza Thrift at Parker and Independence is your next stop. This no-frills thrift store is the sister shop to the Thrift Store and offers an ever-changing selection of clothing, toys, and household finds, all at wallet-friendly prices. It's especially great for stocking up on everyday basics like men's shirts, pajama pants, tanks, and kids' items.

The store is spacious and simple, with helpful staff on hand, many of whom speak Spanish, creating a comfortable shopping experience for bilingual or Spanish-speaking shoppers. While not every visit will uncover a hidden gem, the deals you do find make it worth stopping in regularly.

Whether you're building a wardrobe on a budget, outfitting kids who grow faster than your paycheck, or just browsing for fun, Plaza Thrift is a reliable place to score a few great deals.

3115 W Parker Rd., 972-964-0001
plazathrift.com

FIND YOUR NEW READ AND CUTE GIFT
AT BIBLIOBAR

Bibliobar is the realization of a dream. Owner Chelsea Tresp, a longtime Plano resident and passionate reader, always envisioned owning a bookstore that felt warm, welcoming, and community-centered. Nestled along 15th Street in Downtown Plano, her shop delivers exactly that—an indie bookstore where readers of all ages can connect, explore, and feel right at home.

You'll find a uniquely curated selection of books—from contemporary fiction and memoirs to children's stories and book club favorites. A dedicated kids' nook features comfy seating and space to browse or read quietly. The shop also stocks clever gifts, from themed stickers and bookmarks to slogan hats and handpicked items perfect for any reader. It's the kind of place you'll want to linger, browse, and come back to again.

1018 E 15th St.
bibliobartx.com

TIP

Check their Instagram or website for upcoming author events, story times, and special pop-ups.

STROLL, SHOP, AND DINE
AT THE SHOPS AT LEGACY EAST

The Shops at Legacy East and its northern counterpart, Legacy North, offer one of the most walkable and vibrant destinations in Plano. Positioned on both sides of Legacy Drive, this upscale area is a favorite for locals and visitors alike. With tree-lined streets, easy parking, and pedestrian-friendly crossings, it's perfect for a casual day out or a romantic evening stroll.

Boutiques, beauty salons, and spas are tucked between renowned restaurants like the Capital Grille and Fleming's. Whether you're in the mood for a luxe steak dinner, artisan gelato, or simply browsing fashion and lifestyle finds, there's always something to discover here. There are some great hotels nearby that make it a great place to stay and play for out-of-towners.

During the holidays, the Shops come alive with twinkling lights and festive decor, turning the whole area into a postcard-worthy scene. It's Plano's version of city shopping, without ever leaving town.

Legacy Dr., between Dallas North Tollway
and Communications Pkwy.
shopsatlegacy.com

DISCOVER TRENDSETTING STYLE
AT LEGACY WEST

Plano's most glamorous shopping and dining destination, Legacy West, is often called the Rodeo Drive of the suburbs—and for good reason. Cruise down Windrose Avenue on a weekend and you'll spot luxury cars, stylish shoppers, and a buzz of activity from brunch to nightfall. This is where big-name brands like Gucci, Chanel Beauty, and Lululemon meet chic local boutiques and a world of international cuisine.

Craving French onion soup and Spanish tapas on the same day? You can do that here, and top them off with a craft cocktail or scoop of gelato. At one end, Legacy Hall and the Lexus Box Garden host foodies, music lovers, and families looking for a lively vibe, while the Renaissance Hotel anchors the other with sleek sophistication.

Look up and you might spot model planes near the Boeing offices, eye-catching murals, or Instagram-worthy installations perfect for the younger crowd. And don't miss the fountains. After dark, they put on a colorful light show that adds just a touch of Vegas to West Plano.

Windrose Ave. and 5908 Headquarters Dr., 469-609-1500
legacywest.com

SCORE DEALS OR SELL YOUR OWN CLOSET
AT INDY CLOVER

Indy Clover puts a fresh spin on consignment shopping. This clean, well-organized store lets everyday folks rent a booth for a flat weekly fee and sell their own gently used clothing, shoes, accessories, and home decor—no haggling, no porch pickups, and no Facebook drama. Just be sure to register ahead of time, as spots fill up quickly. It's the ultimate hassle-free alternative to garage sales.

With new booths set up every week, there's always something different to discover. Fridays are popular sale days, and weekends bring fresh finds from new sellers. Whether you're looking for something stylish, unique, or just budget friendly, chances are you'll stumble on a hidden gem for yourself or someone in your family.

The staff is helpful and kind, and the shopping experience feels more like a boutique than a secondhand store. And if you've got a closet full of "someday" outfits or unused decor, why not become a seller yourself? Indy Clover makes it easy.

1941 Preston Rd., Ste. 1008, 817-661-4519
indyclover.com/location/plano

SNAG DESIGNER DEALS
AT CLOSET REVIVAL

If you love labels but not the price tags, Closet Revival is your dream come true. This high-end consignment boutique offers one of the best curated selections of designer fashion in the Dallas area, right here in Plano. From Johnny Was and Lilly Pulitzer to Lululemon, J.Crew, and Eileen Fisher, the racks are filled with fashion-forward treasures at a fraction of retail prices.

You'll find women's sizes ranging from 0 to 3XL, a standout purse wall, and even a full men's section stocked with everything from everyday wear to elevated essentials. Looking for business attire or statement pieces? This place delivers both with organization and style.

It's easy to lose track of time (and your budget!) here because there's just so much to love. Whether you're shopping for work, weekends, or a one-of-a-kind outfit, Closet Revival makes designer fashion accessible and fun.

3405 Midway Rd., Ste. 400, 972-378-9797
closetrevivalplano.com

DRESS UP YOUR LITTLES
AT ANIMAL CRACKERS

For sweet, stylish clothes that make your little one feel like royalty, Animal Crackers in Plano is a must-visit. This charming boutique specializes in baby, toddler, and young kids' clothing with a curated selection that's as adorable as it is unique. From ruffled dresses to dapper little sets, every item here feels handpicked for special moments.

Step inside and you're greeted by friendly staff who go above and beyond to help, whether you're shopping for a holiday outfit, a baby shower gift, or just indulging in a girls' day out with your mini fashionista. It's the kind of place where kids light up, especially when they get to twirl in front of the mirror.

Prices are on the higher end, but the quality and uniqueness make it perfect for gifting or dressing up for memorable occasions.

1900 Preston Rd., Ste. 260, 972-867-4802
animalcrackers.com

BUILD BIG SMILES
AT BRICKS & MINIFIGS

If your household includes a LEGO lover, Bricks & Minifigs is about to become your happy place. This specialty toy store is packed wall-to-wall with new, used, and retired LEGO sets, plus an ever-changing selection of minifigures, bulk bricks, and accessories you won't find anywhere else.

Run by staff who are true LEGO enthusiasts, it's a great spot to nerd out, find that missing piece, or trade in your old sets for something new. Keep an eye out for special sales days that offer great discounts on selected ranges, especially if you're building on a budget.

Whether you're shopping for a kid or a collector, or just want to inspire a little creative play, this locally owned shop is a builder's paradise.

7224 Independence Pkwy., Ste. 332, 972-618-2343
bricksandminifigs.com/plano-tx

TIP

If your LEGO fan is looking for bulk pieces, the store often has bulk sales on set days of the week or month!

MAKE GIFTING MAGICAL
AT LEARNING EXPRESS TOYS & GIFTS

For thoughtful gifts that bring instant smiles, Learning Express Toys & Gifts is a one-stop wonder. From pastel plushies and puzzles to birthday party goodie bags and fun seasonal surprises, this locally owned toy boutique makes shopping for kids more personal without the overwhelm of a big-box store.

Let your child build a birthday bin by filling a container with their favorite picks, making it easy for friends and family to find the perfect gift. The staff is helpful, the options are curated by age and interest, and best of all? Gift wrapping on every purchase. It's hard to beat that!

Whether you're planning an Easter basket or birthday bash, or just need a pick-me-up present, Learning Express offers a personal, hands-on shopping experience with all the convenience of online ordering—plus a little extra magic.

2412 Preston Rd., Ste. 140, 214-499-9009
learningexpress.com/stores/plano

DISCOVER STYLE AND GIFTS GALORE

AT GRIFFIN & GRACE

Griffin & Grace is the kind of boutique that makes shopping feel like a girls' day out, even if you're just popping in solo. Tucked away in West Plano, this locally loved spot is known for its carefully curated racks of clothing, accessories, and gifts that hit the sweet spot between trendy and timeless, with reasonable prices too.

Their secret sauce is how connected they are to their customers. Join their private Facebook group and you'll see new arrivals modeled by real women, often styled with outfit ideas you didn't know you needed. See something you love? Comment to reserve it, and they'll ship it or hold it for easy in-store pickup.

Beyond clothing, Griffin & Grace is a one-stop shop for gift giving. From witty mugs and local Texas gear to college merch perfect for proud parents and grads, they've got something for every person (and every occasion) on your list.

5960 W Parker Rd., Ste. 224, 469-642-3011
griffinandgraceboutique.com

90

ADD A POP OF GLAM
AT BRIANNA CANNON

If you've seen a head-turning headband around town, chances are it came from Brianna Cannon. Located at the corner of Park and Preston, this boutique is a bright and beautiful haven for bold accessories and statement jewelry. The brand's signature headbands have earned a cult following, yes, even among health-care professionals and their patients!

The store itself is as colorful and welcoming as the team behind it, especially Sarah, whose cheerful energy keeps customers coming back again and again. Whether you're popping in for a quick gift or joining one of the fun pop-ups or in-store parties, every visit feels like a celebration.

From game day glam to everyday sparkle, Brianna Cannon offers that just-right piece to elevate any outfit, and it's all available right here in Plano.

1900 Preston Rd., Ste. 155, 469-847-8877
briannacannon.com

TIP

Brianna is most well-known for her signature headbands, which are branded—for sports fans or clubs! You'll be stopped in the street when you wear yours.

DRESS YOUR LITTLES IN STYLE

AT SOUTHERN STORK BABY AND CHILDREN'S BOUTIQUE

For timeless children's clothing with a Southern flair, Southern Stork Baby and Children's Boutique is a must-visit. Located near Park and Preston, this charming shop draws families from all over the DFW area—and once you see the selection, you'll understand why. With over 150 upscale brands for ages 0 to 6, it's a go-to destination for both everyday essentials and picture-perfect outfits.

The boutique shines especially when it comes to stylish options for little boys (which are notoriously hard to find!), along with classic, heirloom-quality pieces for babies and toddlers. The owners are incredibly welcoming and happy to help you find just the right look or wrap up a beautiful baby gift on the spot.

Whether you're shopping for your child or celebrating someone else's, Southern Stork is full of sweet finds you won't see at big-box stores.

5809 Preston Rd., Ste. E-579, 469-814-9786
southernstorkboutique.com

PLAY DRESS-UP
AT DALLAS VINTAGE SHOP

Need a costume? Dallas Vintage Shop has every costume you can imagine and probably 10 more you didn't even think to look for. From the moment you walk in, you're surrounded by an overflowing (in the best way) collection of costumes, accessories, wigs, hats, and props from just about every era and theme imaginable.

Whether you're gearing up for a themed party, Halloween bash, cosplay convention, or theater performance, this store is a gold mine. Think steampunk goggles, medieval armor, flapper dresses, and detailed historical replicas, all under one roof. It's also a fun spot to try things on and be silly, even if you're just browsing.

Prices can be on the higher side, but the quality and selection are unmatched. Come with a vision or just come with curiosity. Either way, you're bound to leave with something unforgettable.

1855 N Central Expy., 972-422-7256
dallasvintageshop.com

93

EMBRACE TEXAS STYLE
AT VAQUEROS WESTERN WEAR

Blink, and you may miss it! Vaqueros Western Wear is in a mall strip store and displays big western appeal the minute you step inside. A family-owned small business with a range that could rival the big chains, Vaqueros Western Wear is a go-to spot in Plano for quality boots, classic hats, and authentic western style.

The knowledgeable and friendly staff at Vaqueros make all the difference, helping you find the right fit whether you're shopping for everyday wear or for a special occasion. With a strong selection for men, women, and kids, this is an easy stop for anyone looking to add a little Texas flair to their wardrobe.

1120 E Parker Rd., #203, 214-704-8838

SCORE AND SELL DESIGNER GOODS
AT KEEKS

If you're looking for luxury, Keeks is your go-to destination in Plano. For over a decade, this locally owned boutique has built a reputation as one of the best spots in the state to shop authenticated secondhand designer goods. Think Louis Vuitton, Chanel, Gucci, and Prada—at prices that make high-end fashion feel a little more within reach.

Owners Kristen and Robert, the wife-and-husband team behind Keeks, have created a trusted experience that blends style, value, and customer care. Their massive showroom is luxe but approachable, dripping in designer finds and filled with everything from vintage Chanel and Louis Vuitton to fun accessories like belts, wallets, and shoes. Whether you're shopping or selling, you'll feel like you've stepped into a fashion lover's dream.

4909 W Park Blvd., Ste. 151, 469-367-0340
keeksdesignerhandbags.com

TIP

Inventory moves fast. Follow them on Instagram! You can also sell your own items to them.

DANCE INTO STYLE
AT SANDY'S DANCEWEAR

For dancers of all ages and stages, Sandy's Dancewear is a go-to destination and worth the trip, no matter where you're coming from. Known for its expert fittings and extensive inventory, this locally loved shop has everything from ballet slippers to tap shoes, leotards to tights, and the perfect pair of pointe shoes.

Parents new to the dance world will especially appreciate the knowledgeable staff, who take the guesswork out of what's needed for class or recital. They understand growing kids and changing sizes, making the experience stress free and spot-on.

Whether you're prepping for your very first dance class or a competitive performance, Sandy's makes sure you leave with the right fit and a little more confidence.

3115 W Parker Rd., Ste. 190, 214-473-6600
sandysdancewear.com

TIP

Call ahead if you're looking for a specific brand or product, or need a set size, to see if they have it in stock or can order it ahead for you.

96

EXPERIENCE A TASTE OF SCANDINAVIA
AT THE WOODEN SPOON

Step inside the Wooden Spoon and you'll feel like you've been transported straight to Sweden, Norway, or Denmark. This beloved Scandinavian shop in Plano is packed with treasures you won't find anywhere else, from crisp cookies and sour gummies to imported jellies, chocolates, T-shirts, books, and traditional gifts. It's a candy lover's paradise and a cultural gem all in one.

The friendly staff is happy to help, whether you're hunting for authentic treats, shopping for a school project, or just curious about Nordic culture. Don't miss the chance to make a cookie wish (yes, it's a thing!) or sample the punch during special events. Upstairs, there's even a cozy space for private gatherings or club meetings.

Yes, imported goods come at a higher price—but the experience, the selection, and the warm welcome make it more than worth it. You'll leave with something sweet in hand and a smile on your face.

1617 K Ave., 972-424-6867
woodenspoonplano.com

HUNT FOR HIDDEN TREASURES
AT PLANO ANTIQUE MALL

If you love the thrill of discovery, Plano Antique Mall is a must-visit stop. Located within a typical Plano strip mall, this massive indoor space is filled with booths from dozens of vendors offering everything from vintage furniture and retro kitchenware to rare collectibles, costume jewelry, and quirky finds you didn't know you needed. It's the kind of place where you can spend hours wandering and still feel like you missed a few corners.

Whether you're a seasoned picker, a weekend browser, or just furnishing your home with something unique, this locally loved spot invites you to slow down and explore. It also occasionally hosts outdoor parking lot sales, where even more treasures spill outside for bargain hunters to browse. The inventory changes often, so every visit promises something new.

6505 W Park Blvd., Ste. 250, 972-424-2995
planoantiquemall.com

98

EXPLORE THE WORLDS
INSIDE MADNESS GAMES & COMICS

Madness Games & Comics is a Plano institution for pop-culture lovers, comic book collectors, and tabletop gamers of all ages. With over 40,000 square feet of merchandise, it's one of the largest comic and game stores in the state and an experience all its own. The walls are lined with everything from the latest Marvel and DC releases to rare graphic novels, manga, action figures, trading cards, and board games for every level of play.

Regulars come for tournaments, artist signings, and demo nights, but even first-timers will feel welcome exploring the colorful shelves and buzzing play space. Whether you're a Dungeons & Dragons die-hard, a Pokémon enthusiast, or just looking for a nostalgic gift, there's something here for every kind of geek and then some.

3000 Custer Rd., Ste. 310, 972-943-8135
madnessgames.com

TIP

The events calendar is always full. It has something for everyone, so be sure to follow it and plan your visit accordingly.

99

JUSGO TO ASIA
WITHOUT LEAVING PLANO

For a taste of Asia, explore Jusgo Supermarket. Beyond groceries, you'll find a lively food court, unique snacks, specialty gifts, health and beauty products, and a bustling weekend energy that locals love.

It's known for its authenticity and is centrally located for regular visits. We love going there for specific ingredients for a new recipe and simply to explore the new and unique products on the shelves or fresh produce that you cannot find anywhere else.

If you're an Asian dessert lover, head to the back of the store to get yours from one of the specialty vendors, pick up a hot meal on the go, or purchase from the freezers to take home.

240 Legacy Dr., Ste. 200, 972-517-8858
jusgosupermarket.com

TREAT YOURSELF
AT CRAVE POPCORN CO.

Teens (and anyone with a snack craving) love to sample everything from classic butter and caramel to creative mixes like dill pickle, spicy buffalo, or birthday cake. There's always something new to try, with special seasonal flavors popping up throughout the year.

Crave is also packed with nostalgic candy, fun sodas, and cute gifts, making it a go-to for picking up treats before a movie night or finding a unique gift for a friend. The staff are always happy to offer samples and help you build your perfect popcorn bag or box.

Do not go hungry here, especially if you have a sweet tooth!

4021 Preston Rd., Ste. 619, 972-608-9900
cravepopcornco.com

TIP

Ask about the "Popcorn of the Month" and check out the gift tins, perfect for birthdays, holidays, or sharing with friends.

Iron Horse
Credit Jennifer Shertzer

ACTIVITIES BY SEASON

SPRING

SUMMER

FALL

WINTER

SUGGESTED ITINERARIES

A DAY OUT WITH THE KIDS!

GIRLFRIENDS' DAY IN PLANO

ARTS AND CULTURE DAY IN PLANO

OUTDOOR ADVENTURES IN PLANO

EPIC DATE NIGHT IN PLANO

INDEX

Plano International Festival
Credit Plano International Festival

Plano African American Museum
Credit Jennifer Shertzer